# Project Illuminae

**MARIUM ZARA**

AURAQ
PUBLICATIONS

Printed:     May, 2021                 Cover Art by:    Bilal Mahmood
Edition:     1st                      Edited by:       Kainat Khalid
ISBN:        978-969-749-112-4
Price:       Rs 850 PKR, $8 US

www.auraqpublications.com | raabta@auraqpublications.com
@AuraqPublications | @AuraqBooks +92-300-0571-530
Printed and Bound by *Passive Printers* - www.passiveprinters.com

아침은 다시 올 거야 어떤 어둠도 어떤 계절도 영원할 순 없으니까

*The morning will come again because no darkness, no season is eternal.*

봄날 (Spring Day)
BTS

# DEDICATION

Often you see this section dedicated to friends, family or even inspirational figures, someone who inspires the writers in creating their works.

But unlike others, I am dedicating this work solely to myself: me of the past, the person I am today and who I will be tomorrow.

And as you read this book, I also want you to dedicate this reading to yourself, for this book may include glimpses from your past, your present and your possible future.

With love,
Marium Zara

# ACKNOWLEDGMENTS

Penning raw emotions down on a piece of paper is scary. What if my words are interpreted wrong? This thought kept knocking at the back of my mind as I decided to unveil my true self, without any filters, through my poetry.

I must acknowledge that lowering my barriers wasn't an easy journey to make. I had to face countless restless nights, tossing on my bed, contemplating whether it was worth it, whether I was worth voicing my life out.

I was scared, scared to be misjudged, misinterpreted or thought off differently by the ones close to me. But why would I restrict myself and fear my own loved ones? If they truly love me, they will always be there for me. This thought gave me the courage, the motivation, and the energy to pick my pen and be myself; to the world, I no longer wanted to hide from.

When giving acknowledgments, I especially want to acknowledge those who introduced me to the harsh realities of life, for my poetry sprouted out of those very experiences that wounded my soul, scarred my existence, and dimmed my being. I am thankful to them for making me the person I am today; for allowing me to realize my true worth and take ownership of my being. I am thankful to them for allowing me to see myself as someone worthy of love, worthy of care and worthy of life.

Here, I would also like to show gratitude towards those who helped me in transitioning to be this fearless poet who no longer wants to hide behind vague acronyms and anonymous posts. They made this journey possible, easier, and bearable for me.

Firstly, I would like to thank Tehreem Soomro, without whom this catalogue of my thoughts would never have existed. Her consistent and continuous support was a significant stepping stone to help this book come to life.

I would also like to thank my editor, Kainat Khalid, for assisting me in putting together this collection. I believe that editing poetry is harder than editing fiction, for only a few can successfully step into your shoes and feel your words through the same lens with which you write them. Her opinions and critique helped me a lot in sharpening my vision and conveying my thoughts more clearly.

I would also like to give credit to Bilal Mahmood (@artsomepasta) for successfully designing my feelings into such an aesthetic book cover. My vision, combined with his creativity, helped me add vibrancy to this book.

Lastly, I would like to thank my parents who have always helped me in broadening my intellectual horizon. Their love and support will always be the prime contributor to my motivation.

Marium Zara<br>January 2nd, 2021

# INTRODUCTION

Introducing someone's book with your words is a burdensome and responsible task that everyone is hesitant to take on. However, at the same time, it is also an honor to be able to introduce you, the readers, to this marvelous creation by someone who has experienced, lived, and felt the words that this book encompasses. It is a well-known fact that an individual's art is an extension of his or herself and the same can be said for Marium. Breaking out of the stereotypes, normative conventions, and societal expectations, Project Illumine is the reflection of an individual who found her own axis to rotate, her own orbit to revolve, and her own light to shine.

Project Illumine has the potential to compel the darkness to submit to the light. It is keen to overpower the season of gloom by unlocking the door to a soft velvety twilight. The book uses the words to liberate thoughts in an artistic and perceptive manner with just the right amount of poetic dose for people who seek artful delectation.

The first chapter of the book, Nigritude encompasses a series of poems that foregrounds the innate darkness within the soul and outside the boundaries of the skin. The chapter comprises memories of loss, preserved in poetry that articulates illustrations of the conscious to the subconscious. The poems are also an intricate collection of memories formed of fuel and flames, igniting a raging inferno of dejection, wistfulness, remembrance, and nostalgia; memories that are as fragile as the wind-chimes, just as tumultuous and just as melancholic. The poems release anger, a moment of justified anger, in the right instant and in situations that have left everlasting scars on the soul.

Umbra is the second chapter of the book. It gives prominence to the fact that darkness and coldness are only a prelude to warmer days. The faith that there is a reason to be hopeful, even if it has never been witnessed. It serves as an assurance that the trail of hope will gradually emerge and the tiny flicker of light against the darkness will soon pave way for the fresh beginnings.

Like the phases of the night, of the moon, of the seasons, we all transform as time passes. We are not in a constant frozen place. That is where this book begins, in a frozen place with only a flame to guide us; that flame is the hope inside of us that someday things will get better. It communicates that the winter is not forever and that spring is around the corner. To reach spring we must fight the cold that has taken shape from our hesitation, insecurities, and vulnerabilities. Poems keep these cold places warm.

When you think you are ready to step onto a road of spring, your inner shadows might obstruct your way. Cold winds might blow your flame. Then remember to be steady. Shadows appear whenever there's the brightest light, just like despair looming whenever there is hope. At that instance, what matters is either if you chose to face the light or the shadow, the moonlight or the dark of the forest. Twilight is around the corner so just hang in there for a moment.

The last part of the book is Twilight, as assured by the starlit night, the long obscured sun rays start to make an appearance. As darkness yields to the light, every colour switches from charcoal to sprightly. Twilight offers the opportunity to rejuvenate and regenerate before the new day arrives.

"I am still not tired though,

I still write," (I am not tired yet 17-18)

Take your lantern in your hands and run towards the morning because the night is not forever, cold is not forever. We learn these things along the way. Taking a flight like a phoenix from the ashes of emotional wreckage into the twilight sky ready to face the morning Sun.

This is Project Illumine. The long journey from disintegration to reconstruction.

*—Samia Inam & Tehreem Soomro*
*Islamabad & New Delhi*
*March 7, 2021*

# CONTENTS

15. Dear D,
16. I used to think that love was smooth sailing
17. Its been a long time since this feeling came into
    place
18. We all wish to be loved
19. Wasted all my life
20. I used to write poetry

# Nigritude

Proclaimed the time was neither wrong nor right.
I have been one acquainted with the night.

—*Acquainted with the Night*
Robert Frost

# 1

My mind is dripping with words,

thoughts that are aching to be written,

to be recorded, to be remembered.

I wonder if my hands will do justice to them.

I wonder, whether my heart can bear them

whether the readers can feel them,

whether the person they need to reach

will see them, and treasure them,

Or just throw them away,

like a penny is thrown in the pond for a wish.


I wonder if my words will be enough.

Whether they will bring you solace,

in this ash ridden chaos that the world has become.

Life that has turned into moments,

simple, aching moments that are hard to feel.

It's like a pendulum;

going through a mundane motion,

With the crisp feel of the illusion of a future.

I wonder if you are waiting,

waiting for an epiphany.

I wonder if my words can be your savior,

whether they can pull you from the ashes,

or from the mundanity,

yet, I know it's a lost cause,

to try and bring life into words that have died.

I have learnt to move forwards,

But, words are words,

Hence, I will keep your ashes, you keep my words.

## 2

I have been feeling this emotion lately,
it's not anger, nor is it sadness.
Maybe it's just numbness, or the feeling
you get when you give up on the things
you once held close to you,
cherished like the dolls you had when
you were just four years old.

The emotions are oozing out like lava.
Anyone even remotely close knows,
just how burnt they'll be if they try to touch,
to feel, or to make me feel.
I have long given up on the doll,
so what's to say I won't give up on you?

3

6

You change

like the season of

Autumn, shedding

each layer

one after another.

i wonder if you'll grow,

new leaves,

or stay barren like me.

4

You'd think there would be beauty

in every little action that took place

as I slowly let go of the past

and greeted the present with a smiling face.

I would try to hold it in,

the small whimpers and despair

and look at the horizon and wonder

whether you would be waiting to repair.

The path is not quite smooth,

with patches to hide the holes

my scathed soul whimpering

to be filled to the brim and be whole.

I wonder sometimes whether you can see

the small tools and pebbles lying around

waiting to be used and un-corroded barely,

to fill the cracks that have been long found.

I thought I would have to fight my way

to be remembered, to be heard.

How foolish of me to think,

you were waiting,

when your actions deferred.

5

Pain is an old friend of mine.

It won't go away anymore.

It has embedded itself,

with a cataclysmic vengeance into this flesh.

Every vein is filled with hatred for the blood,

that moves through it every step.

The world has started to implode,

with the depth of despair that you have left.

You were kind enough to leave this band-aid,

without a shred of alcohol to disinfect.

This wound is going to scar,

with all the pain visible on the body,

I guess I will have to spar,

with my heart that is cocky,

of the pain you left it in,

leaving nothing but anger,

for it to fuel and become a stranger.

to the body, it resides in,

while you leave with a blinding grin.

6

When you left without your shoes.

1

It was not a coincidence or a chance meeting.

There was destiny and fate waiting for greeting.

Whenever there was a voice outside the door,

I would wonder whether the locks would click

and emerging figure greet me like yesterday.

However, it has been more than a decade,

with my eyes stuck to the door,

my ears waiting for the sound of your footsteps.

There is only too much silence that a soul can bear.

It is hard to live in the now,

Your mind wanders to all the ultimatums,

all the horrors, the dreads of the unseen.

However, there was a calmness in this darkness.

I could see so clearly,

as if the light had been switched on.

A light that was visible only to me.

But, what do I do with a light that is only stagnant?

I could try to move with its flow, one step at a time;

but lights have a tendency to diminish,

when you try to brighten the room.

They don't play well with the shadow,

It can consume both, light and dark

like an old friend.

2

It was the spring of year when you had left.

Before, everything used to look alive.

Flowers would judge if you didn't smell them

or held them in your hands, preserving

the little precious aroma that they weft.

It has been more than 365 days,

since someone has smelled them.

As I look at them, I see the withered petals,

gently waiting as if only a day has passed.

The flowers used to make me cry,

made me want to bawl, and crush

the dried petals in my fist,

Like you had crushed the future,

when you sat in that boat of never return.

I am still raising these flags on the poll,

With hope, that they'll show you the way back home.

3

It was the winter of the year when you cried;

cried for your broken dreams,

cried when you missed your chance to breathe.

I would sit on the armrest, patiently,

waiting for my turn to soothe

those long intervals of defeat,

With little gentle touches, and looks;

knowing that expression was better than words.

However, winter is never gentle to the soft,

It bring havoc and destruction with its claws.

I have moved through the cold though.

Yet, your old and worn out shoes still sit,

right next to the door that signified

that you were never to sit,

but to soar.

I wish opening my eyes was easy,

as easy as taking my next breath.

I wish the spring would come back,

there is so much snow to walk through,

but only one shovel to dig it up now.

## 7

I open my eyes, slowly coming back to reality.

The remnants of my dream slowly fading.

The horns that were so real become shadows,

as if they were a trick of my imagination;

letting me know I can still Dream the dreams.

In my dream, I am a knight,

with my sheaths ready to plunge me into these remnant ends.

I stand against this army that you have built.

It screams loud and clear to show strength,

but all I see, is dying valor and unrequited will.

I move forward along this maze of ash and death,

to fight one last time in the name of strength.

Unfortunately, shields can only save you so many times,

until they give up under the weight of the strike.

## 8

He came to see me with his family,

as if one wasn't enough,

to objectify my being

And put me under cuffs.

They decorated me

like a shiny ornament,

Ready to be displayed.

Was I just a body for them,

or a mannequin with which

they could play?

They deflowered my ego,

my independence.

Because it was too much

voice for a woman to be feminine.

I thought only the other gender

were my slayers.

How foolish of me to think,

when my own sisters

were my betrayers.

9

I have been walking for a long time,

in this cold weather.

The snow has become stagnant now,

just like my steps, seizing their motion.

I used to wait days,

in this white layered city,

with its lights fluttering on and off

letting the flow of time known,

as I waited out my promise.

To always wait, and repair.

The air used to be cold,

as cold as a glacier,

about to seize one in its clutches.

I would wear a scarf around my neck,

and those small mittens,

that you thought you lost.

I would blow into my hands,

as I yet waited another day,

because I had promised.

Promised to always wait.

I would stare at the walls,

in front of the bench,

that had become my companion,

during the long days.

Wondering if my regret,

was bigger than mother nature.

If my apology was sincere enough,

to survive the snow.

If my hold on reality strong enough,

to live through my promise.


I have been walking long,

in the shoes of regret.

I have walked alone, I have walked together.

My steps had been singular, however,

Hand in hand, I would feel a little hope.

An imaginary hope, but a hope nonetheless.

In the night sky, I would reach out my hand,

wishing you were here, not up there.

So that I could fulfil the last promise,

not hold on to it.

10

Before the twilight hit the earth,

there used to be an us.

There was a beginning and end to things.

Now, as I move forward, all I see is a maze

with you in the past, me in the present,

with only twilight as our friend.

I wonder if my darkness and your light can merge,

whether we can transcend time and place,

and meet where it all ended.

There is still a ray of light lurking,

about to be extinguished by the darkness,

I hope the moment doesn't falter,

or pass us by.

It has been too long a journey,

for just a moment goodbye.

## 11

Is love an affinity?

or water that drowns,

or is it a fire that burns?


I don't know the answer,

but I know the cries,

that reach my ear,

when someone who loves

loses the other,

in the wake of their fear.

12

I have always lived my life

wondering about your tastes

whether you will find the color blue

or the color green better.

whether you wear sock to sleep.

whether you drink water direct from the bottle.

But the most pressing thought

that always lingers in my mind is

whether you think about me too.

Whether you realize my taste,

my thoughts, and my mind.

How sharing is hard, how words,

that once were easy to vomit

are hard to claw out of my throat.

I wonder if you see that I hate my brows

and every little imperfection

that stares back at me.

I wonder if you think like me,

When you see something that makes you think

'oh, you'd like that.'

or maybe you just don't see at all,

what really is in front of you.

Maybe, that is why my words are tired too

they have long lost their destination,

now aimlessly wandering the horizon,

hoping to reach home,

but how do I tell my heart it's the end,

when it's still stuck at you?

13

He was the artist, she the canvas.

He knew

which colours could bring her to life,

and which could bleed her dry.

She, like many others

trusted his strokes,

to paint her a beautiful colour,

Like a mosaic, put up on display.

Silly of her to think, he would do justice,

instead of bright yellows,

he painted her blue and grey,

instead of gentle strokes.

He splashed black,

as if all she deserves were

monotonous filters.

She still sits, right beside the many

knicks and knacks, and jettisons.

Her colours still not filled.

## 14

These small windows that I used to look out of

seemed much smaller from the outside.

Maybe my vision had become big,

or maybe just real.

I never used to think between the lines

when I looked at my relations.

But the essence of belonging slowly faded away,

as if the shore got swallowed up by the ocean.

Maybe the bond was there to break from the beginning

and me, just a mere catalyst

waiting for the tide to turn

as if I could surf my way through.

Little did I know;

It's not the ocean that drowns you but the tide.

15

In amidst all the ego and pride,

they forgot the path they had led.

The thorns they had pulled

out of each other's bleeding soles.

The small brush to the cheek, subtly

rubbing the neck muscles to make

the day that was to come better

than the one they had to live through.


The pride had told the heart to hold back,

that you're not always supposed to bend,

to fix the irregularities or to just lend

a small hand or a word of love,

or be a breath next to the other

as life slowly went.


However, ego was nuisance.

It lashed out, sneaked up from behind,

and broke what once was cherished.

It struck the thorns so deep into the flesh,

the breath took a long course around,

wandering the old taverns and streets

hoping to find the way back home.


Now, the path was amiss.

the tear had been shed,

feet had moved their course

and lastly, they had stopped.

Stopped at the calamitous turn,

where companions had left the reign

to let the still breath be,

to let the still breath be,

to let still breath breathe...

I'm clustered,

into a plethora of feeling,

and emotions that

I wish I could discard them.

You've been running for so long,

Have you not found your destination?

Your ultimate goal?

You used to love that musical box

with its melody out of sorts,

like a vintage sound.

I used to believe your way might turn

away from your path and

one day, you might stumble

in front of my front door,

smiling crookedly, holding the

melody hidden inside.

But yet another year passes us by,

me, still an emblem of emotions

holding the song,

And you still trying to hide.

## 17

"What if I'll never forget you?"

These words echoed for a long time

in this hazy place I called a brain.

Yet, there he was.

Standing tall and so graciously,

why hadn't he changed with time?

Why for him, time slow and benign.

But for me, cruel and unkind?

He still looked like the day he left,

His eyes as kind as they used to be,

when he would softly murmur,

Gentle touches into my soul.

Whereas, here I was, rugged to the bone,

showing the signs of growth.

Eyes as manic as an addict, to a life

that was much like one of a convict.

I used to live on the memory of hope,

that he wouldn't forget,

me, the one he promised to keep.

In his heart, in his mind,

all throughout the end of time.

Even when I would force my beliefs

of nothing remaining eternal and dying with time.

Then why was I breaking?

Why was his forgetting more hurtful,

than the disease that I had in my brain?

His hand in another's more constricting

than a box for a cluster phobic.

Maybe that was my punishment,

for being ignorant of his feelings.

He probably gave my thoughts away,

just like I gave his love away.

## 18

October.

The month of truth,

Trees shedding their colors;

Showing what lies beneath.

Those brass looking leaves,

each have a story of their own.

Slowing falling down

from those long echoes of branches

shedding themselves to the truth.

Hey October,

Why don't you shed humans too?

Theirs masks are getting too attached for good.

No real is left to see.

Just abstract coloring, no pattern.

Maybe the black and white will be better.

At least there will be no more arrogance.

The clock stopped ticking as it reached 8:14 of January.

Which year it was, seems unimportant now.

It felt like I let go of something precious,

something that made me feel gracious.

People blame others when things go wrong,

but how do you blame others,

when you're the one at fault?

Its easier to blame unhappiness upon others,

harder to realize that the blame lies at home.

It's in those small conversations that led nowhere,

in those overconfident thoughts.

in the never ending fights,

over who was wrong and who was right.

over why there was so little time,

when the other was there all the while.

It was over ignorance and priorities,

over time and its unavailability.

We think the clock can stop if we're content,

Little do we know, the clock doesn't stop ticking,

it goes on, and on, and on.

But why did my clock stop ticking?

Why has it been stagnant?

Like the calm before the storm.

Did it realize its mistakes?

Or did it break a precious death?

## 20

Do I still taste of war?

With my flesh smelling like fresh blood;

my bones like melted wood;

my heart like broken glass,

with pieces scattered everywhere.

Do I still look a nuisance to you?

With my trust in you so high,

my fears like a jumbled up sigh.

My feeling like a joke so funny,

that beats like a resonating melody.

Come on now, don't be shy.

This body is no more feelings and emotions,

it's just flesh and bones acting like a human.

If you look inside, you might find a reason

As to why there are so many complications.

## 21

I wish I was strong enough to hide,

All the scars that you left behind.

but I'm a mere human who resides,

in a world for me that you left aside.

## 22

As I walked through the graveyard,

Looking for ragged old tombstones.

All I could find were dreams and hopes

six feet under like useless cargo.


Looking inside my heart, I wondered,

whether I was also buried there somewhere,

Because it's been too long since I breathed easy,

in this melancholic life that's ever unfair.

# Umbra

*The woods are lovely, dark and deep,*
*But I have promises to keep,*
*And miles to go before I sleep,*
*And miles to go before I sleep.*

*—Stopping by Woods on a Snowy Evening*
Robert Frost

1

Death.

That was the first thing that I thought of,

when I fell from the flight of stairs.

I wondered if I would see the light,

at the end of the road

that everyone talked about.

Light so bright that it would take away,

all my agony, and my breath.

falling with a force of divinity,

every step felt like a step towards eternity.

Slowly, one after another;

hissing over every shattered spear

that pierces into my body.

I reached my destination, with big black door.

It asked me a question 'whom shall pass?'

'Me!' I replied. Not knowing the depth

that the question was asked with.

The door asked me again,

'Whom shall pass?'

I replied again, 'Me!'

Not knowing the severity of the situation,

wondering what it was that I was missing!

The answer? Or the question?

The door asked one last time,

'Whom shall pass?'

I stayed quite, contemplating.

Did I have to go back and be revived?

or merely stay in the hereafter for life.

Could I go back in time?

or just accept my fate and my demise.

Slowly I looked at the door and smiled,

That little flutter of hope finally died,

Because no living can pass the dead.

and I was finally able to pass.

2

The life had been harsh on her,

One after another,

brutal weathers

she would run sometimes,

and crawl the other.

but one thing she knew,

she was a wildflower,

strong enough to handle your trample,

and wild enough to be called a weed.

3

Deeply indebted to those time

when there was nothing but everything,

when you would pull me forward,

clutching my hand tightly,

as if letting go was as close to dying.

I still feel the hard touch, the broken skin,

the callouses of your hand,

despite your hold being long gone.


I used to believe that you would stay,

never letting go, holding on.

However, there's always a way of nature,

you cannot fight it, no matter how much you try,

you always have to shore your boats,

at one point.

I guess you shored too early,

I was not ready to drown.

4

In the throes of circumstances,

In the grueling vicious cycle of ashes,

Still stands, bleeding,

like a butchered statue,

Ready to be cooked,

a hand.

Mere anarchy could not turn

the knight who had given,

his heart, his soul.

His shield, and his sword,

in the name of the heart,

Of *Snow*.

Obstacles were his challenge,

to gain him his title.

But little did everyone know.

She was the prize,

he wanted to own.

Swords crackling,

shields hitting the metal,

he fought his way through,

like a lone man,

with a world full of barrels,

and fell to his knees,

waiting for his gentle

*Snow*, like the ice,

but soft like the petal.

She picked up his hand,

the one covered in blood,

and cradled it in her bosom,

Smiling like the spring,

that he had waited for.

5

The blue hue of the sky,

grey skin of the earth.

The red blood oozing out,

as if the ground is spitting on us.


There was a hope for green,

while the grey took over.

How do you tell the sky,

that black is the new color?

## 6

I confronted my reality,

with my sheaths ready to unravel.

My sword swinging back and forth,

while my shield kept me in its curve.

There were quite a few choices,

waiting to be made into concrete.

Though I wasn't ready, I pushed, I pulled,

I did what I could while I could.

Unfortunate for me, choices were stuck.

In a maze of uncertainty and Oblivion.

I stepped up, and asked my fate,

Whether it knew if I was gonna win this game.

It smiled and told me to walk away,

That the war is only won,

when the fate lets you outwit your own claims.

7

I guess this shred of paper has burnt down.

It once used to contain an amalgam of my memories,

the words were too soft to handle this ferocious climate.

The lines were too blur to create their own path.

The world has been too harsh on this tedious existence.

It has taken away, those silvers of hope from under the guise.

Little stagnant clovers that used to shine as bright as the sky.

I guess I should give up the hope of ever reuniting,

with the memories and hope that once were cherished

like a Cheshire cat purring because of content.

Maybe these intricate roads with burnt flames will give way.

So that this dying soul can breathe one last breath.

8

46

I live in this meliorism

that things will change,

You will come,

And spring will rain.

I have been holding on for so long

I have forgotten how to let go,

these small soft hands with callouses

so deeply ingrained in the skin.

I used to tremble every time you let go.

My hands empty and looking

for a home that was too far to hold.

We have been drowning for so long

that I doubt you'll realize

when the breath becomes air

and the air makes you numb.

I only hope that even when we go cold

I'm still holding on tightly,

to your hand, calloused and broken.

## 10

I wish I could escape.

To a place that has no gates.

No entrance and no exit.

A place that is secluded,

away from mankind,

with its garbage and its noise.

I wish you are with me in that seclusion,

that you are alright in that world,

no marks on your fragile body,

No needles sticking in.

No shallow breath taken forcefully,

or a pain so intense that it shatters

the glass that I've created

to keep the reality away.

I have been looking inside the room.

Waiting to see,

your hairless head on display.

Your closed eyes,

and your spotted hands.

The blood in your arms has turned to blue.

I wonder how to fix it.

Only to find out,

that it is impossible to be done.

So, I take a tentative step towards you,

hoping the glass will keep you safe

but deep down my head knows,

the more I try to save it,

the more and more it will break.

So, I let the glass shatter and,

turn to broken pieces and shards.

Because in my heart, I know.

You're more happier with eyes closed,

Then staring at nothing at all.

## 11

There are a lot of victims of my poetry.

Reason behind my every syllable,

The witty words and unfinished sentences,

leading on and on to a never achievable end.

I wonder what leads me to make you,

The subject of my words,

Whether knowingly or obliviously,

Maybe it is those feelings that I try to bury

Or those scars that I try to burn.

Maybe the words are my screams,

And my exclamations, my questions.

There are a lot of victims of my poetry

And one of them is myself.

## 12

I have been too scared to give shape to words,

in fear of them getting out into the world,

and turning into something other than words.

This world has a way of changing;

little to enormous, big into small.

I never know if what I say is going to stay,

or will it take a shape of a beast,

changing the tide with its speech.

I wish that words were like water;

so that they could wash away everything,

all the horrible deeds that happen,

or might happen in the future.

Unfortunately, they are like a desert,

hot during the day, icing cold during the night.

We never know which phase to expect.

Maybe that's why they say,

choose your words carefully.

## 13

I'm strong, a brick.

I keep telling myself,

as I stare at the reflection in the mirror.

as I frigidly sit.

But the world has knocked me down,

The bones have broken even more,

like how the glass shatters,

when you throw it with force.

I've come to a place

where there is no light shining.

There's a door with a blank room.

I thought I could enter it,

and not feel the cold.

However, the darkness is too great,

for the warmth to grow.

Stay strong, be strong.

I keep telling the mirror,

I keep telling myself.

## 14

May we reach those far away stars,

not even knowing,

the path on which we are.

It may look like they are far and high.

But the distance is only long,

if you don't know the sky.

I hope there is a path,

to those far away star.

Because I don't know how long,

I can look for the radars.

## 15

I have been staring at the blank wall

with my tear stricken face;

as I slowly, but surely give up.

Give up on the hope I clutched on to,

held so tightly that my hands got calloused.

Each nail broke into my flesh,

showing the sheer force it took to take the next breath.

It needed to be done, to be free.

To not feel burdened by the weight of

something, that was not mine to keep.

It was a ticking time bomb,

to keep my breath steep.

Just so you would feel better in your skin.

Yet, as I moved a step forward,

one breath came easy, then the next.

Next thing I knew, I was filled with so much,

I felt never so full.

I hope I never have to empty myself into someone again,

But who am I kidding?

The first was a choice,

the second will be fate.

## 16

Small hands accompanying

Big dreams drowning,

What were we supposed to do?

when the world was frowning?

You held me close

like I was your shield,

not knowing it was me

That was your leash.

17

I want to break these chains

these shackles that you've put on me.

I'm not as strong as you think.

I can't bring myself to say,

this reality that I face.

I used to look at the stars and see,

all my worries wash away and gleam.

But now, everything is bleak.

This sky that used to bring me peace.

Now, it's filled with horrors and screams.

I try to speak, mumble even.

Unfortunately, sounds are hard to reach.

The ears of the ones who need to hear.

Unfortunate for me, I don't know;

How to fight back the power of stones

That these deaf ears throw at me.

Or I wouldn't be in these shackles,

Trying to break free, hoping to show;

the resilience left in this body.

## 18

I have been walking aimlessly,

with no destination in mind.

You have been hovering over,

waiting, just out of my sight.


I sit by the shore gazing,

Looking at the waves as they hit,

Not knowing you are beside me,

waiting for your chance to sit.

"You've been waiting a while," I say.

Your smile, "hasn't been forever yet."

## 19

It has been exactly 3 hours, 43 minutes, and, 25 second.
Each moment has felt like it's never going to end.

I was told that counting numbers backwards is the key,
but the letters have left my brain before I can even speak.
The soft tapping of the clock tells me that time is passing.
When my boats have lost their sails and have declared
sinking.

My eyes catch the last light, the last flicker of your gaze;
before it was gone for good forever, never to return.

I wonder if my brain can store the scene.
Or whether it will bleed with an aggression.
The road is very risky but it's okay.
I have survived a trio of sixties,
I can definitely survive eternity.

## 20

As I read through these old letters,

the ones that I wrote to myself.

I see the old me, trying, trying to be free;

trying to speak, speak on the blank sheets,

as if they'll give the answers

that the mind cannot repeat.

I trace each ink spot, wondering if it'll dry out

with the change in temperature.

Just like life did, when the seasons changed their color.

One leaf at a time.

The letters are floating in my head

"Why?", "How?", "Can I?", "Should I?"

I pluck each word out and write a new letter.

Why not today? Why not now?

How do I live? How do I soar?

Can I wait? Can I move on?

Should I give up? Or

should I hold on?

Vulnerable.

That's what we are

as we lay out our hearts.

In front of people bare,

not knowing if they'll care.

We think we are aware,

Of the thundering storms

And the little affairs

that brew when we wear,

our hearts on our sleeves and stare,

in their dazed eyes, wondering

if they'll repair.

All the broken pieces and dare,

To put one piece of themselves there,

where there's a hollow,

asking for a spare.

## 22

Hoping for a way,

as I stray away from the bay,

you have left me at

to rot and decay.

But I defray and convey,

all my difficulties and dismay,

so that you relay,

when you go to heaven to stay,

all the cruel things

that humans do to feel gay.

23

These emotions rule me no more.

I have packed them away in a suitcase close.

There are so many answers that you give me of

but all I hear are excuses for your foul.

I knew it was in vain, trying to live on like nothing's wrong,

with the knowledge that I was fighting a losing war.

I fight my absolution daily, hoping to stay strong

knowing the fight, keeping my dignity in thaws.

But all it does to me is break,

shattering me slowly, no sympathy in its stance.

My heart in clutches, tightening its grips

to push me off the edge and breaks me to fall.

Nights getting colder and sad,

knowing the dark coming closer to engulf,

these sad moments that are surrounding me

the suitcase shouting at me to break free,

telling me to run and hide from the uncanny.

Me, holding on to the little pieces

Of what I used to be, fighting still.

Knowing if I let go, I'll be letting me down,

just like everyone did to myself.

She asked me to tell her what I was thinking.

How could I answer her when I didn't know myself,

the turmoil that was inside my mind,

the wreck that my thought were making of my decisions.

I look at her old eyes,

stare at those wrinkles that have taken shape.

Maybe it was just the old age,

or maybe it was the tiredness.

I wanted to ease her mind with my words,

but nothing would come out,

as if my words were dying a painful death,

and were taking their last breath.

I took her old rusty hands in mine and squeezed,

giving her the only words that were left in me.

I wonder sometimes,

if she understood my unspoken words.

Understood better than this page,

that I keep filling with haze,

not knowing if it'll stay,

and relay what I was thinking,

once.

# Twilight

*A tree's leaves may be ever so good,*
*So may its bark, so may its wood;*
*But unless you put the right thing to its root*
*It never will show much flower or fruit.*

*—Leaves Compared With Flowers*
Robert Frost

1

I've been feeling empty for quite some time now.

These days are too long to survive,

the chaos that's in my mind.

I wonder sometimes; when we will meet again.

When the nights will turn to days,

and the days will turn to nights.

We've got different nights and mornings to wake up to.

Yet, I know.

The sun that is rising in my sky

just set in yours,

bringing to me a sense of melancholy and content.

Knowing, that a part of your life,

will always be connected to mine.

2

A twilight moment.

A moment I yearn for.

a singular moment

when I could have everything.

I could have the sun,

but I could also have the moon.

I could have the night,

But also the afternoon.

but mostly, I could have the light,

while still keeping my nigritude.

3

I used to think,

I was not good enough.

How foolish of me to think,

that God would play me dirty.

When he took the pain that

would have come my way,

if I had obtained,

what was not mine to attain.

## 4

There was little inclination in bounds,

no amount of time could fix it.

I chased the clock as it ticked,

not knowing what it was taking away.

Forged an iron armour knowing

leather couldn't keep me at bay

From the wrath of this storm

that clock had ticked my way.

My brain is a maze of ideas

but with little inspiration to say,

What it means is such a puzzle,

it takes decades to relay.

I write my words,

not knowing if they will stay,

Bringing me understanding

like they bring me to a different maze.

5

She had very shallow awakenings,

Stagnant, like the waves,

waiting for the tide to turn.

She had waited a long moment,

staring at the excruciatingly slow

tick of the time, as it stroke 13,

Not the perfect number.

but to her, it was, perfect.

it meant she could move,

out of the illuminae of brazen assurances

Into the abyss she had missed.

She knew she had to leave,

this abysmal immortal fear,

and the cocoon she had created,

but who was to say she could survive,

the bright incandescent of hope.

Yet, there she was, striving beyond belief,

One step before the other, looking at the clock,

As it finally strike 13:01,

her new perfect number.

6

I am not tired yet,

tired of writing about the past,

about the monster under my bed,

about the tapping of the rain on my window,

about the flickering of street lamp.

They used to scare me, frighten me even.

I would hide under the canopy,

Or take shelter under your wings.


However, it has been ages since the dawn,

of the day you left,

leaving me with an unmade bed.

I still move however.

With winds that are faster than the rain.

Streets that are filled with wain,

And broken wings filled with pain;

they don't even have life to move.

I am still not tired though,

I still write.

I wonder sometimes,

whether the past lives in me,

or I bring it to life on these pages.

Whatever the case is,

the future should worry,

because words are a world,

not easy to diminish, they linger

hold on, and reside till we diminish.

7

*74*

So I ran in the darkness.

The darkness: my light.

For others, it was blind,

for me, it was my lantern,

lighting up my sky.

I knew the path was steep

but I was already in too deep.

Giving up would be bleak

when all I wanted to do

was to soar and be out of reach.

8

That cold weather, with its tranquil subtlety

slowly eased that ache I had in my stomach.

I couldn't hold my head up high

Maybe it was because of those whimsical fears

Or maybe just timid-ness in my stance.

I can still remember that autumn leaf falling on my head

Its color so orange, that looking at it hurt

as if my vision would break it

and all would be ash and dust

though, it didn't falter, standing resilient.

Maybe it wanted me to see faith

or maybe just hope

that I would fall,

but not fall down at the same time.

9

Pain is a friend I have known,

for years and years long like the stories foretold.

It knows how to reside,

And how to trample,

Yet, it sits calmly,

Waiting for you to cradle,

like a child who hurts his knee

And runs to his mother to find a retreat.

So, don't be scared, the scars heal.

They tend to hurt less with time.

But make you strong like steal.


The blood gets cleaned, so no hatred reside.

But what about the pain?

The one that makes you cry?

Maybe the pain is the growth.

The bearer of epiphanies.

Letting you know,

The hurts was just a breeze

and the scar was just a show,

the real battle was not to fight,

but to be left to grow.

The wounds that this flesh has gained

will reside like an emblem,

for the world to see the reign

that a human with pain

contains inside their body as they live,

each day unrestrained.

She had reached a milestone,

there were going to be no more tragedies in her wake.

He had turned her into a tragic novel,

with chapters of anguish and heart break.

It had taken one mere hit

for the climax to come.

Yet, as she stared in his cold and lifeless eyes,

all she could see were her broken pieces.

Her defiled and un-scrumptious being.

Her scalp razed with harsh tugs,

her nails like a mosaic that lost its touch.

She knelt and picked up the grubs

of her shards, and put them together

in the front pocket of her scrubs

as she left the little hole he had pushed her in

not as a defeated woman,

but as an unyielding warrior.

## 11

There are many flowers in the meadow

but only one catches your eye.

You pick at its beauty

not knowing it has a horns at its side.

People realise too late,

that flowers are made to be looked at.

Not to be picked or plucked

but to stand beautiful with grace.

## 12

I have lived with a name that is not mine,

but keeping it like its owner.

I move through this maze of life,

holding things dear that are foreign.


The world has not been forgiving,

punishing me for what I was unaccountable;

telling me I was a nuisance to think,

that it was okay to be different,

in a maze that only knows consonants.


I still stood resilient,

fighting the flow of variations,

with my crackling bones fighting me,

telling me their contingent demise.

"Why must you fight?"

but my name was on the line.


Was a single word so strong?

That it could bring a *Qaum,*

to its knees and perform,

brutalities, and bloodshed,

like it was a game of norms.


The world is still cruel,

Making me hide my name,

As if the waiting monsters are feudal.

Yet, just like foreign things,

My name is my wings,

While you try to depose it,

I spread and expose it.

13

Waiting for the roads to open,

to walk the journey unknown.

I don't know, what I'm supposed to do

when everyone I know is gone.

I want to slip away silently,

not waking the guards,

But these chains make sound

enough to awake the dead.

I hold my hands tightly

together, looking ahead.

There is no destination,

only a path that is to take.

I want to run, I want to hide,

because I know what's at stake.

You will keep me, you will bind,

But you can never force your mind

On my mere flesh and body,

to be your servant, and your key,

when I have a mind that is strong,

enough to say no to your moral decrees.

## 14

For we were breathing so soundly
I bet they thought we were asleep.
But nobody checks that those sound breaths
are the calm winds after a hazy storm;
Those closed eyes, running from the waters of reality.
Those eyelashes fluttering;
Trying to hide as much pain as possible.

Nobody said it was going to be easy,
to run from your problem.
But how does one ignore the arrows
that are embedded in one's being?
How does one move on to great things
when the first step is still to be taken.

Winners are those who see the end,
before they begin,
and don't let the tethers stop them,
or slow them down.
Because even a small step is a step nonetheless.
And if one can move forward with arrows,
they can definitely move till the end.

*Dear D,*

1

*Dear D,*

You have been my addressee

To a lot of words,

that are never sent.

You are my calm,

when there's too much unrest.

I write like a manic,

trying to break free,

but how do I do that,

when your love, free,

and tender is a bequest

Onto me?


2

*Dear D,*

You've been a subject of my poetry,

my words, my worth.

Why wasn't I enough?

Was there some subtraction in my love?

Or some deception in your trust?

I knew I had changed,

but so had you.

We were no longer kids,

who didn't know,

the brutal life that awaited,

as we grew.


3

*Dear D,*

I knew it was a pain,

to let the love stem,

into a harsh cry of bane.

But you were waiting patiently,

waiting, to see,

if I would collapse,

under the weight that I myself put

on my wounded wings,

ready at the mark,

for if I even for a second stumbled,

you would be there with open arms.


4

*Dear D,*

I'm sorry,

I'm sorry I put such a heavy burden;

burden of my love in your lap.

Hoped you would swallow

all my brutal hits,

wait me out,

stay patiently,

as if I hadn't put the key to the door

in your hand,

and asked you myself to leave,

even if without words.

Yet, you stayed; hoping.

Silly thing is a hope.

You learnt the lesson by leaving,

I learnt it by watching the door close.


5

*Dear D,*

It has been years,

since I've written down the follies,

the abstract that I put

in the lives of the ones I loved.

People pen down about who hurts them.

I used to do that too,

break my words, and make them bleed.

Put the hurt that I felt over your shoulders,

try to ease my soul, and bring peace.

Yet, today, as I see my life,

the one who hurt me was always me,

the one putting the leash around my neck,

were always my own hands.

The pain that I felt was of my own making.

Others, only the promotors,

me, my own destroyer.

16

I used to think that love was smooth sailing,

gliding over the ocean. One wave at a time.

But I as grew older,

It made more sense why people cried,

when they said they fell in love.

Love is not smooth like a feather,

its to deal with brutal weathers,

hurtful words, and unrequited tethers.

I had a preconceived notion,

Of what love would be like.

having a significant other,

who understood all my signs.

I never realized love was a friend,

Cradling me in her arms as I cried,

when things got too hard to reply,

with words that were filled with whines,

for a love that was a lie.

## 17

Its been a long time since this feeling came into place

There didn't used to be calmness before the havoc.

There was always some sudden emotion waiting

Just behind the curtains, about to surface

The air has made it soar up in the sky

Making the mind numb, and ready for impact.

The meteor that you foresaw,

has already hit the ground

Bringing with it a shell of a person

That is hard to understand.

We sit across from one another daily, wondering

If that spark was only a means for an end.

That the conversations that we had

only took place for us to be here

Pretending that everything is just the way we left.

I still look at the old photographs,

wondering if you're happy

With another me that will never be me.

Whether I left you with pain, or an idea.

I'm burning the past today,

with all the sad parts insides.

There will be no trace of our friendship left in the sky.

So, when you look at the night sky tonight,

know that you're forgiven,

For all the boulders that you threw at me

In the name of love and friendship.

Make sure you wear a coat tonight,

it will be the coldest you will feel.

With my ache going, and going, and gone.

## 18

We all wish to be loved,

to be cared for, to be treasured.

But why do we not love ourselves?

Our imperfections? Our scars?

And our broken hearts?

Our endurance to not give up.

Maybe our hearts are not made that way

Maybe, they have to go through trials

through harsh calamities and savage brutalities

to be considered mighty.

But why not we, the bearers

of a hidden treasures

give our heart the crown it deserves?

A crown made by our resilience,

our hard work and persistence.

Maybe the world wants us to go down,

So that when we rise,

We know the journey was not to be perfect,

but to be beautifully imperfect.

# 19

Wasted all my life

trying to make

people see my worth.

Never realised,

I was more important

than the world.

## 20

I used to write poetry,

to cleanse my mind of bad thought.

But what to write

when there is nothing in my mind?

Shall I write about those faces,

that I imagine each day of people I've never seen?

Or shall I write about the sky?

that's forever sunny and hot.

Or maybe about that pencil

that you took and never gave back.

There so many things to write about

with only the subject being in turmoil.

The mind is perfectly alright,

with its logic and expression ready to conquer,

while the body is worn to the bone,

and falling a parts at its steams.

I wonder if anyone will read my poetry,

if it was about that girl that no one saw.

Or about those unruly hair,

that you could never straighten.

Maybe I'll write a new poem,

with just s flicker of hope.

That this won't be the first,

nor will it be the last.

# ABOUT THE AUTHOR

Marium Zara was born in Islamabad in 1998 and has lived all her life in the Capital city. She graduated with a degree in English Language and Literature from International Islamic University Islamabad in 2020. She has been writing poetry for years; however, Project Illuminae is her first published work.